The Power Within

Transform Your Mind, Transform Your Life

By

Peter Kattan

Book Bound Press

https://web.facebook.com/BookboundPress/

Preface

Every one of us has a reservoir of untapped potential—a hidden force that, when harnessed, can transform not only how we think but also how we live. This book, *The Power Within: Transform Your Mind, Transform Your Life*, is an invitation to embark on a transformative journey. It is a guide to discovering and embracing the immense strength, resilience, and possibility that lie within you. Through deliberate shifts in perspective, intentional practices, and a commitment to growth, you can unlock your true potential and create a life that aligns with your deepest aspirations.

The inspiration for this book came from years of observing human resilience in the face of adversity and the profound changes people experience when they dare to embrace new mindsets. Whether working with individuals overcoming personal challenges, hearing stories of triumph against the odds, or reflecting on my own journey, one truth became evident: change begins from within. The external world—with its trials, uncertainties, and distractions—may challenge us, but our response to it is shaped entirely by the power of our minds.

The Power Within is designed to serve as both a guide and a companion. Each chapter is carefully crafted to build upon the last, leading you through a process of self-discovery and growth. From uncovering your inner strength to learning how to set intentional goals, challenge limiting beliefs, and cultivate mindfulness, this book offers practical tools, strategies, and stories to inspire action. These principles are not abstract theories; they are grounded in real-life experiences and accessible techniques that anyone can apply to achieve meaningful change.

Throughout these pages, you will find moments of reflection, challenges to old ways of thinking, and opportunities to envision a future defined by possibility. This is not about chasing perfection or adhering to a rigid self-help formula. Instead, it is about empowering you to take ownership of your life and to understand that transformation is a journey—one that celebrates progress over perfection and growth over stagnation.

The themes explored in this book—resilience, gratitude, mindfulness, and intentional living, among others—are universal. They transcend age, background, and circumstance, reminding us that the pursuit of a fulfilling life is a shared human endeavor. Whether you are at the beginning of your self-improvement journey or seeking to refine the practices that have already brought you success, this book is for you.

As you read, I encourage you to approach each chapter with an open mind and a willingness to engage. Take notes, reflect on the exercises, and, most importantly, apply what resonates with your unique experiences and aspirations. Transformation is not a passive process; it requires effort, courage, and patience. But the rewards—a life of purpose, fulfillment, and resilience—are immeasurable.

To those who have contributed to the ideas within these pages—the friends, mentors, and individuals who shared their stories of struggle and triumph—I offer my deepest gratitude. Your courage and wisdom have been instrumental in shaping this book, and your journeys stand as a testament to the power of the human spirit. Finally, to you, the reader: this is your journey. As you turn the pages, may you find the inspiration, tools, and encouragement to harness *The Power Within*. Your potential is boundless, and your capacity for growth is extraordinary. Now is the time to transform your mind and, in doing so, transform your life.

Peter Kattan   December 2024

Introduction

Life can be a real rollercoaster, right? Some days, it feels like we're swimming against a tidal wave of challenges. But here's the thing: the quest for personal growth has never been more crucial. Tapping into that inner strength isn't just some trendy self-help slogan. It's about digging deep and finding the resilience that's been hanging out inside you, just waiting for a chance to shine. This book? It's your ticket to a transformative journey—a chance to uncover the incredible potential you've got locked away.

Imagine waking up every morning feeling pumped, ready to tackle whatever life throws your way. Visualize yourself shaking off those pesky limiting beliefs, welcoming change like an old friend, and building a mindset that pushes you toward your goals. Sounds dreamy, right? But it's totally doable for anyone willing to dive into their own self-discovery.

As you flip through these pages, you'll stumble upon the idea of inner strength—this natural power that's been chilling inside you, just waiting to be unleashed. You'll pick up some cool techniques to boost your resilience, inspired by real stories of folks who've faced tough times and come out on top. These tales? They're like little lights guiding you, proving that challenges can be stepping stones rather than roadblocks.

You'll get the lowdown on the magic of a growth mindset—how your thoughts can totally shape your reality. There'll be practical tips to help you think positively, flipping your perspective and, ultimately, your life on its head. Setting clear goals? That'll become your jam, giving you the energy to push yourself forward. You'll even make visualizing your success a daily habit, firing up your motivation and keeping you locked in on your dreams.

But here's the kicker: transformation isn't just about setting goals. It's about facing those pesky limiting beliefs head-on. Together, we'll dig into those mental barriers and kick them to the curb, rewriting your story to match your true potential. Through inspiring transformation tales, you'll see the magic that happens when you shift your beliefs.

Change? It's gonna happen, folks. In this exploration, you'll learn to embrace it. With some handy strategies for adapting and thriving in new situations, you'll find strength in the unknown. Personal stories will show you the beauty of stepping outside your comfort zone and the richness that comes with it.

Mindfulness will become your sidekick as you learn to be present. You'll discover practical exercises to weave mindfulness into your daily grind, boosting your emotional resilience and helping you connect deeper with yourself and the world. This fresh awareness will crank up your gratitude game, letting you soak in the little joys that often slip by unnoticed.

Nurturing healthy habits? Oh, you'll get the scoop on that too. You'll learn how habits form and the steps to create and stick with positive routines. Your habits will lay the groundwork for your future, helping you grow in ways you never imagined.

Relationships? They're a big deal in personal growth. You'll explore how to build meaningful connections that lift you up. By embracing vulnerability, you'll discover the strength in being open, forging deeper bonds that enrich your life.

And let's not forget self-care. It's gotta be a priority in your transformation. You'll define what self-care means for you and see just how much it can boost your well-being. Personal stories will drive home the point that you can't pour from an empty cup.

You'll also get into affirmations, making them part of your daily routine to help shape your thoughts and beliefs. You'll craft personalized affirmations that resonate with your goals, and you'll see the magic as they start to manifest in your life. We won't shy away from the fact that failure is part of the journey; we'll embrace it as a stepping stone to resilience. Inspirational stories of people bouncing back from setbacks will show you just how strong the human spirit can be.

As you reflect on your journey, celebrating your progress—no matter how small—will become essential. Acknowledging your wins will boost your motivation and create a positive cycle that pushes you toward even bigger successes.

This book isn't just a guide; it's your buddy on this wild ride of self-discovery and transformation. Each chapter is a stepping stone, bringing you closer to the powerful, resilient person you're meant to be. So, are you ready to tap into that power within and change your mind, your life, and maybe even the world? Your adventure starts now.

Table of Contents

Chapter 1

Discovering Your Inner Strength

Life, in all its unpredictability, often feels like a rollercoaster ride—full of exhilarating highs and daunting lows. One moment, you're gliding smoothly along, and the next, you're confronted with challenges that feel as overwhelming as a Midwestern thunderstorm. But here's the silver lining: nestled deep within you is a reservoir of power and resilience, just waiting to be tapped into. Together, we're going to embark on a journey to uncover your inner strength.

Let's start by defining what inner strength truly means. It's not merely about physical prowess or sheer willpower; it's a profound ability to confront life's adversities head-on. Think of it as your internal compass, guiding you through life's stormy seas. It's that unwavering voice inside you that whispers, "You've got this!" even when everything around you feels chaotic. Inner strength is cultivated through self-awareness, emotional intelligence, and the firm belief that you can rise above any situation life throws your way.

Now, let's explore some practical techniques to help you tap into that resilience. The first technique I want to introduce is mindfulness. It may sound sophisticated, but at its core, mindfulness is simply about being present in the moment. When life feels like it's spiraling out of control, take a moment to pause. Breathe deeply. Feel your feet firmly planted on the ground beneath you. This small act can serve as an anchor, helping you clear the mental clutter and regain focus.

Next, let's discuss the power of reframing your thoughts. Instead of telling yourself, "I can't do this," try shifting your perspective to, "I'm learning how to do this." That subtle change in language can unlock doors you never knew existed. It's akin to flicking on a light switch in a dark room—you suddenly illuminate all the possibilities waiting for you.

Visualization is another potent technique worth exploring. Imagine yourself overcoming the challenges you face. Picture it in vivid detail. What does success look like? How does it feel? Engaging your senses in this way is like rehearsing for a big performance; the more you practice in your mind, the more confident you'll feel when the moment arrives.

Let's also take a moment to recognize the importance of support. Surround yourself with people who uplift and inspire you. Share your struggles and victories with them. Think of it as having a cheering squad on the sidelines, encouraging you every step of the way. Even the strongest athletes rely on coaches and teammates to help them reach their full potential.

Now, let's get real for a moment. Life is going to throw some tough challenges your way. But here's the encouraging news: countless individuals have faced adversity and emerged stronger on the other side. Take J.K. Rowling, for example. Before she became a household name, she was a single mother living on welfare, grappling with depression. Rather than allowing those challenges to define her, she tapped into her creativity and resilience, ultimately gifting the world with the beloved Harry Potter series.

Consider Oprah Winfrey's journey as well. She faced unimaginable hardships in her early life, from poverty to abuse. Yet, through it all, she discovered her inner strength. Oprah transformed her pain into purpose, using her experiences to fuel her passion for helping others. Her story is a testament to the incredible power of resilience.

These stories serve not just as inspiration but as proof that you, too, can overcome whatever life throws your way. Each challenge you face is a stepping stone to greater strength and wisdom.

So, what's the takeaway here? Your inner strength is like a muscle—it grows stronger the more you use it. Embrace mindfulness, reframe your thoughts, visualize your success, and lean on your support system. And when you feel like you're at your lowest, remember the stories of those who have risen from the ashes.

Now, let's take a moment for reflection. What challenges are you currently facing? How can you apply these techniques to your life? Grab a pen and jot down your thoughts. You're on the brink of something amazing.

As we continue this journey, remember this: your inner strength is a wellspring of power that's always within reach. The journey to discovering it is just as important as the destination. Embrace the process, celebrate your progress, and know that you are capable of transforming your mind and, in turn, transforming your life.

You've got this!

Building Resilience Through Self-Awareness

As we delve deeper into discovering your inner strength, let's focus on the crucial role of self-awareness. Self-awareness is like the compass that helps you navigate through life's challenges. It's about understanding your thoughts, emotions, and behaviors and how they influence your actions. When you cultivate self-awareness, you gain insight into your strengths and weaknesses, enabling you to respond to situations with clarity and intention.

To enhance your self-awareness, consider incorporating journaling into your daily routine. Set aside a few minutes each day to write down your thoughts and feelings. Reflect on your experiences, both positive and negative. Ask yourself questions like, "What did I learn today?" or "How did I respond to that challenge?" This practice not only helps you process your emotions but also allows you to identify patterns in your behavior. Over time, you'll develop a deeper understanding of yourself, which is essential for building resilience.

Another effective way to boost your self-awareness is through mindfulness meditation. Find a quiet space, close your eyes, and focus on your breath. As thoughts arise, acknowledge them without judgment and gently return your focus to your breath. This practice helps you become more attuned to your inner landscape, fostering a greater understanding of your emotional responses and thought patterns.

Emotional intelligence is another vital component of inner strength. It involves recognizing and managing your emotions and understanding the emotions of others. When you develop emotional intelligence, you can respond to challenges with empathy and compassion, both for yourself and those around you. This skill not only enhances your relationships but also empowers you to navigate difficult situations with grace.

To cultivate emotional intelligence, practice active listening. When engaging in conversations, give your full attention to the speaker. Avoid interrupting or formulating your response while they're talking. Instead, focus on understanding their perspective. This practice not only strengthens your connections with others but also helps you become more aware of your own emotional responses.

Embracing Vulnerability

Let's take a moment to talk about vulnerability. Many people view vulnerability as a weakness, but in reality, it's a powerful source of strength. When you allow yourself to be vulnerable, you open the door to authentic connections and personal growth. It takes courage to share your struggles and fears, but doing so can lead to profound transformation.

Consider the story of Brené Brown, a researcher and author known for her work on vulnerability and shame. Brené's journey began when she realized that her fear of vulnerability was holding her back from forming meaningful connections. Through her research, she discovered that embracing vulnerability is essential for building resilience and fostering a sense of belonging.

To embrace vulnerability in your own life, start by sharing your experiences with trusted friends or family members. Open up about your challenges, fears, and aspirations. You may be surprised by the support and understanding you receive. Remember, vulnerability is not about oversharing; it's about being authentic and allowing others to see the real you.

Additionally, practice self-compassion. Treat yourself with the same kindness and understanding you would offer a friend.

When you encounter setbacks or make mistakes, remind yourself that it's a part of being human. Embracing self-compassion allows you to acknowledge your feelings without judgment, fostering resilience in the face of adversity.

The Power of Gratitude

Another powerful tool for discovering your inner strength is gratitude. Practicing gratitude shifts your focus from what's lacking in your life to what you already have. This shift in perspective can significantly enhance your resilience and overall well-being.

To cultivate gratitude, consider starting a gratitude journal. Each day, write down three things you're grateful for. They can be as simple as a warm cup of coffee in the morning or a kind gesture from a friend. By consistently acknowledging the positive aspects of your life, you'll train your mind to focus on abundance rather than scarcity.

Incorporating gratitude into your daily routine can also be as simple as expressing appreciation to those around you. Take a moment to thank a colleague for their support or tell a loved one how much they mean to you. These small acts of gratitude not only strengthen your relationships but also reinforce your sense of connection and belonging.

The Importance of Setting Goals

As you continue on your journey to discover your inner strength, it's essential to set meaningful goals. Goals give you direction and purpose, serving as a roadmap for your personal growth. When you have clear objectives, you're more likely to stay motivated and resilient in the face of challenges.

Begin by identifying what truly matters to you. What are your passions? What do you want to achieve in your life? Once you have a clear vision, break your goals down into manageable steps. This approach makes your aspirations feel less daunting and allows you to celebrate small victories along the way.

For example, if your goal is to improve your physical health, start by setting achievable milestones. Perhaps you could aim to walk for 20 minutes a day or try a new healthy recipe each week. As you make progress toward your goals, you'll build confidence and reinforce your inner strength.

As you pursue your goals, remember to be flexible. Life is unpredictable, and sometimes plans change. Embrace setbacks as opportunities for growth and learning. When you encounter obstacles, ask yourself, "What can I learn from this experience?" This mindset shift can transform challenges into stepping stones on your journey.

Visualizing Your Success

Visualization is a powerful technique that can help you tap into your inner strength. When you visualize your success, you create a mental image of achieving your goals. This practice not only boosts your confidence but also prepares your mind for the challenges ahead.

To practice visualization, find a quiet space where you can relax and focus. Close your eyes and take a few deep breaths. Picture yourself accomplishing your goals in vivid detail. What does it look like? How do you feel? Engage all your senses as you imagine this success. The more real it feels, the more empowered you'll become.

Visualization can be particularly effective before facing a challenging situation, such as a presentation or a difficult conversation. By mentally rehearsing your success, you'll approach the moment with greater confidence and clarity.

Celebrating Progress

As you navigate your journey of self-discovery and resilience, don't forget to celebrate your progress. Acknowledging your achievements, no matter how small, reinforces your inner strength and motivates you to keep moving forward.

Create a "success jar" where you can drop in notes about your accomplishments, positive experiences, or moments of growth. Whenever you're feeling discouraged, take a moment to read through these notes. They'll serve as a reminder of your resilience and the progress you've made.

Additionally, consider setting aside time for self-reflection. At the end of each week or month, take a moment to review your goals and accomplishments. Reflect on what you've learned and how you've grown. This practice not only helps you stay focused on your journey but also fosters a sense of gratitude for the progress you've made.

The Journey Ahead

As we wrap up this exploration of discovering your inner strength, remember that this journey is ongoing. Life will continue to present challenges, but you now have the tools and techniques to navigate them with resilience and grace.

Embrace mindfulness, cultivate self-awareness, practice gratitude, and set meaningful goals. Allow vulnerability to be a source of strength, and visualize your success as you move forward. Most importantly, celebrate your progress and acknowledge the incredible power that resides within you.

You are capable of transforming your mind and, in turn, transforming your life. Every step you take on this journey is a testament to your inner strength. So, take a deep breath, embrace the process, and know that you are not alone. Your inner strength is always within reach, waiting for you to tap into it.

You've got this!

Chapter 2

The Mindset Shift

You know that feeling when you've got a fire burning inside? That's your growth mindset waiting to blaze. Seriously, having a growth mindset is like putting on these magical glasses that let you spot opportunities while everyone else is busy staring at obstacles. Ever been there? It's that little twist in how you see things that opens up a whole universe of possibilities.

Picture this: you're at the foot of a mountain. Most folks look up and think, "No way I'm climbing that!" But not you. With a growth mindset, you're like, "Bring it on!" You see that mountain as a challenge, a chance to scale new heights, learn, and grow. You genuinely believe that with a bit of grit and determination, you can make it to the top. This belief isn't just some pipe dream; it's grounded in the idea that you can develop your skills, adapt to whatever life throws at you, and rise above the muck.

So, how do you get this growth mindset rolling? Let's dive into some solid strategies to help you think positively. First off, embrace challenges like they're your best buddies. Instead of running away from tough situations, lean into them. Ask yourself, "What can I learn from this mess?" When you hit a wall, don't let it define who you are. See it as just another step on your journey. Remember, every successful person has stumbled and fallen. It's all about how you bounce back.

Another killer strategy? Surround yourself with positivity. Yeah, I'm talking about those peeps who lift you up and inspire you. You know the type—the friends who cheer you on and see your potential even when you're doubting yourself. Seek them out! And don't forget to be that uplifting friend, too. Positivity spreads like wildfire!

Now, let's chat about self-talk. You might not realize it, but the way you talk to yourself is a big deal. When you catch yourself spiraling into negative thoughts, flip that script! Instead of saying, "I can't do this," try "I'm learning and growing." That little switch can totally change your outlook and unlock doors you didn't even know were there.

So, what's the big deal about mindset anyway? Well, your mindset shapes your reality in ways you might not even notice. It affects how you see the world and your place in it. If you believe you can improve, you'll take action to make it happen. But if you think you're stuck, guess what? You'll stay stuck. Your beliefs create your reality.

Let's break this down a bit more. Think of your mindset as a lens you look through to see life. If that lens is fogged up with doubt and negativity, you're gonna struggle to see the good stuff. But when you wipe that lens clean with a growth mindset, suddenly, opportunities pop up everywhere. It's like walking into a room bursting with potential. You'll spot paths you never noticed before, doors you never thought to open.

And here's the kicker: when you shift your mindset, you shift your life. You start attracting positive experiences and people. You become more resilient when challenges come knocking. Even when life throws you curveballs, you'll find you can handle them with style and strength.

Let's take a moment to look at some real-life examples. Think of J.K. Rowling. Before she became a literary superstar, she faced rejection after rejection. But did she let that stop her? Nope! She used those setbacks as fuel to keep writing. Her growth mindset kept her going, and look where it led her! She didn't just change her life; she transformed the lives of millions of readers around the globe.

Or how about Thomas Edison? That guy famously said, "I have not failed. I've just found 10,000 ways that won't work." That's the essence of a growth mindset right there. It's all about persistence, resilience, and believing that every experience is a lesson.

Now, let's get personal for a sec. Think about your own life. What challenges are you dealing with right now? How can you tweak your mindset to see them as opportunities? Maybe you're wrestling with a new job, a tricky relationship, or a personal goal that feels out of reach. Whatever it is, keep this in mind: you've got the power to change how you see things.

Here's a practical exercise to help you along the way. Grab a journal and jot down a challenge you're facing. Then, list three ways you can tackle it with a growth mindset. For example, if you're feeling swamped at work, instead of thinking, "I can't handle this," flip it to, "What skills can I develop to manage my workload better?" Writing it down can really help you commit to that mindset shift.

As you go through this process, be kind to yourself. Growth isn't a sprint; it's a marathon. It's totally okay to trip up along the way. Celebrate those small wins! Every time you challenge a negative thought or embrace a new opportunity, you're flexing that growth mindset muscle.

In conclusion, the power of a growth mindset is massive. It's not just about thinking happy thoughts; it's about believing in your ability to grow and change. It's about viewing challenges as stepping stones instead of roadblocks. By nurturing positive thinking and understanding how your mindset shapes your reality, you can flip your life upside down in ways you never imagined.

So, take a deep breath, my friend. Embrace this journey. You've got the power within you to shift your mindset and create the life you want. Remember, every day is a fresh chance to grow, learn, and rise above. You've got this!

Now, let's dive deeper into what this all really means. The truth is, a growth mindset isn't just some trendy buzzword. It's a game-changer. It can completely reshape how you approach life. Think about it: when you view challenges as opportunities, you're more likely to take risks. You're more likely to step out of your comfort zone. You're more likely to try new things. And that's where the magic happens.

Ever had that moment when you tried something new and it totally paid off? Maybe it was a hobby you picked up or a job you applied for even though you felt underqualified. Those moments? They come from a growth mindset. You see, it's all about having the courage to take that leap, even when you're scared.

And let's not forget about the role of failure. Ugh, failure. Nobody likes it, right? But here's the thing: failure is not the end of the world. It's just a part of the journey. When you have a growth mindset, you understand that failure is a stepping stone to success. It's a chance to learn, to adapt, and to come back stronger. Just like that saying goes, "Fall seven times, stand up eight."

You might think, "Okay, that sounds great in theory, but how do I actually put this into practice?" Good question! It's all about consistency. Start small. Set little goals for yourself that push you out of your comfort zone. Maybe it's speaking up in a meeting or taking a class in something you've always wanted to learn.

And remember, it's not just about the big wins. Celebrate those small victories! Did you try something new today? High five! Did you challenge a negative thought? Boom! That's progress. Each of these moments builds your growth mindset muscle.

Let's talk about feedback, too. Ever get defensive when someone critiques your work? Yeah, it's a natural reaction. But with a growth mindset, you start to see feedback as a gift. It's not a personal attack; it's an opportunity to improve. When someone offers constructive criticism, take a step back and think, "How can I use this to grow?"

And hey, don't forget to reflect. At the end of each day, take a moment to think about what you learned. What challenges did you face? How did you respond? This reflection helps you internalize the lessons and reinforces that growth mindset.

You know what else is important? Setting a vision for yourself. Where do you want to be in a year? Five years? Ten years? Having a clear vision helps guide your actions and decisions. It gives you something to strive for. And when you hit a bump in the road, that vision can help you stay focused on your goals.

Let's not overlook the power of gratitude, either. It might sound cheesy, but practicing gratitude can seriously shift your mindset. When you focus on what you're thankful for, it's harder to dwell on the negative. Try keeping a gratitude journal. Each day, write down three things you're grateful for. It can be as simple as a sunny day or a good cup of coffee. This practice helps you cultivate a more positive outlook.

And remember, it's okay to ask for help. Nobody's an island, right? Surround yourself with a support system—friends, family, mentors—who can encourage you and hold you accountable. Sometimes, just having someone in your corner can make all the difference.

Now, let's circle back to those examples we talked about earlier. J.K. Rowling and Thomas Edison didn't just have growth mindsets; they also had resilience. Resilience is like that secret sauce that helps you bounce back from setbacks. It's what keeps you going when the going gets tough.

Think about your own resilience. When was the last time you faced a setback? How did you respond? Did you wallow in self-pity, or did you pick yourself up and keep moving forward? Building resilience takes practice, just like building a growth mindset. It's about developing that inner strength to keep going, no matter what.

And let's be real for a second: not every day is gonna be sunshine and rainbows. Some days will suck. You'll feel overwhelmed, frustrated, and ready to throw in the towel. But that's when your growth mindset comes into play. It's what helps you push through those tough times. It reminds you that it's okay to struggle, but it's not okay to give up.

As you navigate through life, remember that growth is a journey, not a destination. There's no finish line. You'll always have room to grow and learn. Embrace that! Be curious. Ask questions. Seek out new experiences. Life's too short to play it safe all the time.

And hey, don't forget to have fun along the way! Life's an adventure, after all. Laugh at your mistakes. Share your journey with others. You never know who might be inspired by your story.

So, as you wrap your head around this whole growth mindset thing, keep in mind that it's not about perfection. It's about progress. Every little step you take counts. Each time you challenge yourself, each time you push through a tough moment, you're building that growth mindset.

In the end, it all comes down to this: you have the power to change your life. You have the ability to shift your mindset and embrace challenges. You can create the life you desire. So go out there, take that leap, and watch as your world transforms. You've got this!

Chapter 3

Setting Intentional Goals

Alright, let's jump right in, shall we? Setting goals is a lot like planting seeds in your life's garden. You wanna know what you're planting, where it's going, and how you're gonna nurture it. Without that clarity, those seeds could end up lost in the weeds. You gotta be super clear about what you want to achieve. So, what does success look like for you? Is it landing a new job, adopting a healthier lifestyle, or finally writing that book you've been dreaming about? The clearer you are, the more focused your energy becomes. Think of it like flipping on a spotlight in a dark room—suddenly, everything's visible, and you can see the path ahead.

Now, let's chat about a nifty little framework called SMART goals. Ever heard of it? It's a total game-changer, I swear. SMART stands for Specific, Measurable, Achievable, Relevant, and Time-bound. Each piece of this puzzle is crucial for setting goals that actually stick.

First up, let's talk specifics. Instead of saying, "I wanna get fit," how about "I wanna run a 5K in three months"? That's way more specific, and it gives you a clear target to aim for. Next, make it measurable. You gotta track your progress. How will you know you're getting closer? Maybe you plan to run a little farther each week or keep tabs on your time.

Then, there's achievability. This one's a biggie. You don't wanna set yourself up for failure right outta the gate. It's like trying to leap over a skyscraper when you can barely jump over a puddle. Set goals that challenge you but are still within reach.

Now, let's keep it relevant. Your goals should align with your bigger life vision. If you're gunning for a promotion at work but really wanna start a bakery, well, that's a mismatch. Make sure your goals resonate with your passions and values. Finally, time-bound. Give yourself a deadline. "I wanna run that 5K by June 1st." It creates urgency and keeps you accountable.

Alright, let's shift gears a bit. Visualization—now that's where the magic happens. Picture this: you're standing at the finish line of that 5K, the crowd's cheering, and you're crossing that line with a huge smile plastered on your face. Feels good, doesn't it? Visualization is like a dress rehearsal for your success. It amps up your motivation and keeps you on track.

Take a few moments each day to close your eyes and imagine yourself achieving your goals. See it, feel it, breathe it. The more vivid your visualization, the more your brain believes it's possible. It's like training your mind to recognize success before it even happens. You're laying the groundwork for your journey, one mental picture at a time.

So, let's recap, my friend. Clarity is your compass. SMART goals are your roadmap. And visualization? That's your fuel. Combine all three, and you're on your way to transforming your dreams into reality.

Now, here's a little exercise for you: Grab a piece of paper and jot down one goal you wanna achieve. Make it SMART. Write down how you'll measure it, why it matters to you, and when you plan to accomplish it. Then, take a few moments to visualize yourself achieving that goal. Picture the sights, the sounds, the feelings. Let it sink in.

You got this! Remember, every step you take toward your goals is a step toward a more fulfilled life. Embrace the journey, and keep that inner strength shining bright. You're not just setting goals; you're creating a life you love. So go on, set those intentions, and let's get to work!

But wait, there's more! Let's dig deeper into the nitty-gritty of goal-setting. It's not just about writing down what you want. Nah, it's about crafting a plan that gets you there. Think of it like building a house. You wouldn't just throw some wood and nails together and hope for the best, right? You'd need a blueprint. Same goes for your goals.

Start by breaking your main goal into smaller, bite-sized chunks. If you wanna run that 5K, maybe your first step is to run a mile without stopping. Then, build up to two miles, then three. You get the idea. Each little win is a stepping stone, and it keeps you motivated.

And don't forget to celebrate those small victories! Treat yourself when you hit a milestone. Maybe it's a new pair of running shoes or a nice dinner out. It's all about rewarding yourself for the hard work you put in.

Speaking of hard work, let's talk about the inevitable bumps in the road. Life happens, right? You might miss a workout or fall off track. It's all good. Don't beat yourself up over it. Just get back on the horse. Remember, it's a marathon, not a sprint. Consistency is key, but so is being kind to yourself.

And hey, accountability can be a game-changer too. Share your goals with someone—a friend, family member, or even a social media group. When you put it out there, it's like you're adding a layer of commitment. Plus, you can lean on them for support when the going gets tough.

Now, let's chat about mindset. This is where things can get a bit tricky. Your mind can be your best friend or your worst enemy. Ever notice how that little voice in your head can sometimes be a total jerk? You know the one—doubting you, telling you that you can't do it. You gotta flip the script on that negativity.

Practice positive affirmations. Tell yourself you can do it. "I'm capable. I'm strong. I'm gonna crush this goal." Sounds cheesy? Maybe. But it works. Your brain starts to believe it, and suddenly, you're not just dreaming—you're doing.

And let's not forget about flexibility. Sometimes, you gotta pivot. Maybe your original goal doesn't feel right anymore, or life throws you a curveball. That's okay! Adjust your goals as needed. It's not a failure; it's just a course correction.

Now, let's touch on the power of community. Surround yourself with people who lift you up. Join a running club, a writing group, or whatever floats your boat. Being around like-minded folks can spark inspiration and keep you motivated. Plus, it's way more fun to share the journey with others.

Oh, and speaking of fun, don't forget to enjoy the process. Goals are great, but the journey is where the real magic happens. Embrace the ups and downs. Learn from the struggles. They're all part of the ride.

Now, let's dive into the importance of reflection. Set aside some time to check in with yourself regularly. What's working? What's not? Are you still passionate about your goal? Reflecting helps you stay aligned and make necessary adjustments.

And here's a little secret: sometimes, the path to your goal can lead to unexpected opportunities. Keep your eyes peeled for those. Maybe you'll discover a new passion or meet someone who inspires you. Life has a funny way of surprising us when we least expect it.

Let's not forget about the role of gratitude. Practicing gratitude can shift your perspective. Instead of focusing on what you haven't achieved yet, take a moment to appreciate what you have accomplished. Celebrate your progress, no matter how small.

And hey, don't be afraid to dream big. Go ahead, think outside the box. What's your wildest goal? Maybe it's running a marathon or starting a nonprofit. Whatever it is, let that dream fuel you.

So, to wrap it all up: setting intentional goals is about clarity, crafting a solid plan, and embracing the journey. It's about celebrating the little wins, being kind to yourself, and staying flexible. Surround yourself with a supportive community, reflect on your progress, and practice gratitude.

You've got the tools you need. Now, it's time to take action. Grab that paper, write down your goals, and start visualizing your success. You're not just setting goals; you're building a life you love.

So, what are you waiting for? Get out there and make it happen! You've got this! Remember, every step you take is a step toward a brighter future. Let's do this!

Chapter 4

Overcoming Limiting Beliefs

You know what really gets in our way? The stuff we tell ourselves. Seriously, it's like there's this little gremlin in our heads spouting off all kinds of nonsense. "You're not good enough." "You'll never succeed." Ring a bell? These are limiting beliefs, and let me tell ya, they can be more stubborn than a mule stuck in the mud. But here's the kicker: you can absolutely kick those beliefs to the curb! So, let's get into how you can spot 'em, challenge 'em, and even flip your life upside down in the process.

First things first, let's shed some light on these pesky limiting beliefs. They come in all shapes and sizes, but some are just plain common. Maybe you've caught yourself thinking, "I'm too old to start something new," or "I'll never be as successful as my friends." These thoughts can sneak up on you like a thief in the night, robbing you of your confidence and potential. Often, they stem from past experiences, societal expectations, or even what others think. The key? Recognize 'em for what they are—just thoughts, not facts.

So, take a sec to jot down any limiting beliefs that pop into your head. Don't hold back; let it all spill out. This is your moment to confront those inner saboteurs. Once you've got your list, you're ready to challenge 'em.

Now, how do you tackle that? One killer technique is reframing. It's kinda like flipping a pancake; you just turn it over to see the other side. For example, instead of saying, "I can't do this," try saying, "I haven't learned how to do this yet." That tiny shift opens up a whole world of possibilities. It reminds you that growth is a journey, not a destination.

Another powerful strategy? Question the validity of your beliefs. Ask yourself, "Is this belief based on facts or feelings?" More often than not, you'll find those beliefs are built on shaky ground. Challenge 'em with evidence. If you think you're not good enough, dig up some past achievements and remind yourself of your capabilities. You've done great things before, and guess what? You can do 'em again!

And hey, let's not forget the magic of visualization. Picture yourself overcoming that belief. See yourself succeeding, thriving, and soaking up the glow of your achievements. Visualization is like a dress rehearsal for your mind; it gears you up for the real deal.

Now, let's chat about some inspiring folks who've tackled their limiting beliefs head-on. Take Sarah, for instance. She was a single mom stuck in a dead-end job, convinced she'd never go back to school. But after some soul-searching and reframing her thoughts, she realized her age didn't define her potential. She enrolled in community college and graduated with honors! Now, she's not just supporting her family; she's thriving in a career she loves.

Then there's Mark, who always thought he'd never run a marathon. He believed he wasn't athletic enough. But with some encouragement from friends and a solid training plan, he pushed past those beliefs. He trained hard, and guess what? He crossed that finish line, and it wasn't just a race; it was a testament to his newfound belief in himself.

These stories remind us that transformation is totally possible. It's about breaking free from the chains of self-doubt and stepping into your power. Your beliefs shape your reality, so why not choose beliefs that empower you?

As you work on overcoming your limiting beliefs, remember to be patient with yourself. Change doesn't happen overnight. It's like planting a seed; it takes time to grow. Celebrate the small wins along the way. Maybe you spoke up in a meeting when you usually wouldn't, or you tried something new that scared you. Each step forward is a victory worth acknowledging.

So, what's next? Here's a little exercise for ya. Take your list of limiting beliefs and choose one to focus on. Write down three reasons why that belief isn't true. Then, craft a new empowering belief to replace it. For example, if your limiting belief is "I'm not creative," you might replace it with "I'm learning to express my creativity every day."

Keep this new belief close to your heart. Repeat it daily, especially when those old thoughts try to creep back in. Over time, you'll find your mindset shifts, and those limiting beliefs will lose their grip on you.

Now, let's take a step back and think about why these limiting beliefs are so sticky. They often feel like they're woven into the fabric of who we are. But the truth is, they're just stories we've been telling ourselves. Stories that can be rewritten. It's like a movie script that's gone off the rails; you can always go back and change the plot.

Think about it—when you were a kid, you probably believed in all sorts of wild things. Maybe you thought you could fly if you just jumped off the right swing. As we grow up, we tend to lose that childlike wonder and start buying into these limiting beliefs. But what if we could flip the script? What if we could bring back that sense of possibility?

And let's be real for a second—life's too short to let these beliefs hold you back. You've got dreams, aspirations, and a whole lot of potential just waiting to burst forth. So why let some old, dusty beliefs keep you in a box?

Let's talk about the power of community, too. Surrounding yourself with positive, supportive people can do wonders for your mindset. It's like having a cheerleading squad that lifts you up when you're feeling low. Share your goals with them, and let their encouragement fuel your journey.

Ever heard of the saying, "You are the average of the five people you spend the most time with"? It's true! If you're hanging out with folks who uplift you, you're way more likely to break free from those limiting beliefs. But if you're surrounded by negativity? Well, that's like trying to swim upstream in a river full of rocks.

Now, let's get back to that exercise I mentioned earlier. Choose your limiting belief and dig deeper. Why do you think it's true? Is it based on something someone said to you once? Or maybe a mistake you made in the past? The more you dissect it, the more you'll realize it's just a flimsy excuse holding you back.

Once you've challenged that belief, visualize your new empowering belief in action. Picture yourself living it out in your day-to-day life. See yourself taking risks, trying new things, and thriving. Visualization isn't just a feel-good exercise; it's a way to train your brain to embrace new possibilities.

And hey, let's sprinkle in some humor here. Ever watch a motivational speaker who's all sunshine and rainbows? Yeah, they make it sound easy, but we know it's not always a walk in the park. Life's messy, and so is growth. You might stumble, trip, or even fall flat on your face. But that's okay! It's all part of the process.

Now, let's chat about setbacks. They happen to everyone, and they can feel like a punch to the gut. But remember, a setback is just a setup for a comeback. It's an opportunity to learn, grow, and reassess. Instead of letting a setback reinforce your limiting beliefs, use it as fuel to propel you forward.

Think of it this way: if you were trying to learn how to ride a bike, you wouldn't give up after the first fall, right? You'd get back up, dust yourself off, and hop back on that bike. The same goes for life. Keep pushing through those setbacks, and you'll find yourself stronger on the other side.

Now, let's bring it all together. Overcoming limiting beliefs isn't a one-and-done deal. It's a journey, a process, and it takes time. But every step you take is a step toward freedom. Embrace the discomfort that comes with growth; it's all part of the beautiful adventure of becoming who you're meant to be.

So, go on—challenge those beliefs, reframe your thoughts, and let your story of transformation unfold. You've got this! Remember, you're not alone on this journey. We're all in this together, and every small win counts.

Keep pushing, keep growing, and never forget that you have the power to rewrite your story. You're not defined by your past or by what others think. You're a work in progress, and that's something to celebrate.

Now, go out there and show those limiting beliefs who's boss! You've got the tools, the mindset, and the determination to make it happen. So, what are you waiting for? Get out there and start living your best life!

Chapter 5

Embracing Change

Change is as certain as the sunrise, my friend. It's the one thing in life you can count on. Whether you're ready for it or not, change is gonna come knockin' at your door. And here's the kicker: it doesn't care if you've got plans or if you're comfy in your routine. The world keeps spinning, and we gotta learn to dance along with it. So, let's dig into this idea of embracing change, and I promise, by the end of this, you'll be feelin' a whole lot more equipped to tackle whatever life throws your way.

First off, let's chat about the inevitability of change. Think of it like the seasons. You know how winter eventually gives way to spring? That's change, my friend. It's the natural rhythm of life. The trees shed their leaves, the flowers bloom, and we, too, must adapt to the shifting landscape around us. Life isn't static; it's a river that flows, sometimes gently, other times with a rush. If you resist it, you might just find yourself stuck in a muddy bank, feeling frustrated and out of sorts. But if you learn to flow with it, oh boy, the possibilities are endless!

Now, I get it. Change can be downright scary. It can feel like standing at the edge of a cliff, looking down into the unknown. But here's the thing: every leap into the unknown is an opportunity for growth. You've got to embrace that fear and let it fuel your fire instead of extinguishing it. Picture this: every time you step outside your comfort zone, you're like a seed pushing through the soil, reaching for the sun. It's not easy, but the transformation that comes from it is worth every ounce of effort.

So, how do we adapt and thrive in these new situations? Well, it starts with a shift in mindset. Instead of seeing change as a threat, view it as an adventure. Ask yourself, "What can I learn from this?" or "How can this make me stronger?" When you reframe your perspective, you open up a world of possibilities. It's like putting on a pair of rose-colored glasses—suddenly, everything looks a little brighter.

One practical strategy is to embrace flexibility. Life is unpredictable, and the more rigid you are, the harder it's gonna be to bend without breaking. Think of a tree in a storm; the ones that sway with the wind are the ones that survive. So, practice being open to new ideas and experiences. Say "yes" more often, even if it feels a little uncomfortable. You might just find yourself in a situation that changes your life for the better.

Another powerful tool in your arsenal is to build a support network. Surround yourself with people who uplift you and encourage you to step outside your comfort zone. Share your fears and aspirations with them. You'd be surprised how many folks are right there with you, feeling the same way. Lean on each other, share stories, and celebrate the little victories together. Remember, you're not alone in this journey.

Let me share a little story from my own life. A few years back, I found myself at a crossroads. I was in a job that felt more like a cage than a career. Every day was the same old grind, and I was starting to lose my spark. One day, I decided enough was enough. I took a leap of faith and left that job to pursue something I was passionate about—writing. It was terrifying, let me tell you. I didn't know if I'd make it, but I knew I had to try. I embraced the unknown, and while it wasn't all sunshine and rainbows, I learned so much about myself along the way. I discovered resilience I didn't know I had and met incredible people who inspired me to keep going. That leap changed my life in ways I couldn't have imagined.

Now, I'm not saying every change will be easy or that you won't face challenges. Life has a funny way of throwing curveballs. But it's how you respond to those challenges that defines your journey. When faced with uncertainty, remember that you have the power to shape your reality. You can choose to adapt, learn, and grow. And that's where the magic happens.

Here's a little exercise for you: take a moment to reflect on a time when you faced change. What did you learn from that experience? How did it shape who you are today? Write it down. Acknowledge the strength you found in that moment. It's easy to forget how far you've come, but reflecting on your past triumphs can be a powerful motivator to face future changes head-on.

As you navigate through life, remember to stay curious. Embrace the unknown like a child exploring a new playground. Ask questions, seek knowledge, and never stop learning. The world is full of surprises, and every new experience can teach you something valuable. So, whether it's a new job, a move to a different city, or a shift in relationships, approach it with an open heart and an eager mind.

In closing, I want you to remember this: change is not the enemy. It's a part of life's beautiful tapestry. Embrace it, learn from it, and allow it to transform you into the person you're meant to be. You've got this! With every step you take into the unknown, you're not just surviving—you're thriving. So go on, take that leap, and trust that you have the power within to navigate whatever comes your way. The best is yet to come, my friend!

Chapter 6

The Art of Mindfulness

Mindfulness, folks, is like a secret weapon for the soul. It's about being present—truly present—in the moment, and it's got some serious benefits. When you practice mindfulness, you're tuning into the here and now, letting go of the past and not worrying about the future. It's like putting on a pair of glasses that lets you see the beauty in everyday life, even in the simplest of moments. Imagine sipping your morning coffee, feeling the warmth of the mug in your hands, and savoring that first sip like it's the best thing you've ever tasted. That's mindfulness in action.

Now, let's talk about the benefits. Mindfulness can reduce stress, improve focus, and even boost your emotional resilience. You see, when life throws curveballs—and trust me, it will—mindfulness helps you bounce back. It's like having a sturdy life raft in a stormy sea. Instead of getting swept away by your emotions, you learn to ride the waves. You develop a deeper understanding of yourself and your reactions. This isn't just some fluffy concept; it's a game-changer for your mental health.

But how do you get started? Well, I'm glad you asked! Incorporating mindfulness into your daily routine doesn't have to be complicated. Let's break it down into some practical exercises that'll have you flexing your mindfulness muscles in no time.

First off, let's try the "Five Senses Exercise." Find a quiet spot—could be your living room, a park, or even your car (just not while driving, alright?). Take a deep breath and focus on what you can see, hear, smell, taste, and feel. Maybe you notice the vibrant colors of the leaves outside or the gentle hum of the refrigerator. This simple practice grounds you in the present and helps you appreciate the world around you.

Next up, we've got mindful breathing. Sounds simple, right? Well, it is! Just take a moment to close your eyes and focus on your breath. Inhale deeply through your nose, hold it for a second, and exhale slowly through your mouth. Repeat this a few times. If your mind starts to wander—and it will— gently bring your focus back to your breath. It's like training a puppy; it takes patience, but you'll get there.

And don't forget about journaling! Grab a notebook and jot down your thoughts and feelings. Reflect on your day, your experiences, or even your dreams. This practice not only helps you process your emotions but also encourages you to be present with your thoughts. It's a great way to check in with yourself and cultivate a deeper awareness of your inner world.

Now, let's chat about how mindfulness fosters emotional resilience. Life can be a rollercoaster, and when the ups and downs come, it's easy to feel overwhelmed. But mindfulness teaches you to observe your feelings without judgment. Instead of getting swept up in anxiety or frustration, you learn to acknowledge those emotions and let them pass like clouds in the sky. You might say to yourself, "I'm feeling anxious right now, and that's okay." This shift in perspective is powerful. It gives you the strength to face challenges head-on.

Think about it like this: when you're mindful, you're not just reacting to life's challenges; you're responding with intention. You develop a toolkit for handling stress and adversity. Instead of feeling like a pinball being bounced around, you become the player, navigating the game with grace and purpose.

You know, I once had a friend who was going through a tough time. She lost her job and felt like the world was crashing down. Instead of wallowing in despair, she turned to mindfulness. She started meditating daily, practicing gratitude, and focusing on what she could control. Over time, she found clarity and strength she didn't know she had. It was like watching a flower bloom after a long winter. That's the power of mindfulness, my friends.

So, as you embark on this journey of mindfulness, remember to be patient with yourself. It's not about perfection; it's about progress. Each small step you take is a victory worth celebrating. Embrace the process, and don't be afraid to explore different techniques that resonate with you. You've got this!

Now, let's wrap it up with a little visualization exercise. Picture yourself in a peaceful place—maybe it's a serene beach or a cozy cabin in the woods. Take a moment to imagine how it feels to be there. What do you see? What do you hear? How does your body feel? Allow yourself to soak in that tranquility. This mental retreat can be a powerful reminder that you can find peace within yourself, no matter what chaos surrounds you.

Mindfulness isn't just a practice; it's a way of life. It's about embracing the present moment and all its beauty. So, as you go about your day, remember to pause, breathe, and appreciate the little things. You have the power within you to transform your mind and, in turn, transform your life. And that, my friend, is the true essence of mindfulness. Keep shining bright!

Chapter 7

Building Healthy Habits

Hey there! Let's get real about habits. They're the sneaky little things that shape our lives—like the hidden puppeteers pulling our strings. Good habits can boost us up, while bad ones can drag us down into the muck. So, how do we get those good habits rolling? Let's break it down and figure out how to tap into that inner strength of yours.

First up, let's touch on the science of habit formation. Now, I know what you're thinkin': "Science? That's for the nerds!" But hang tight! Knowing the basics can actually help you understand why we do what we do. Habits come from something called the "habit loop," which has three parts: cue, routine, and reward.

Imagine this: you stroll past a bakery (cue), and bam! That heavenly smell of fresh bread hits you (hello, temptation!). You can't help yourself and decide to grab a treat (routine). That warm, buttery croissant makes you feel all warm and fuzzy inside (reward). Over time, this loop gets embedded in your brain, making it easier to repeat the behavior. It's like creating a path in the woods—the more you walk it, the clearer it gets.

But here's the kicker: bad habits are tough to shake, but you can build positive habits using the same loop. Instead of a croissant, let's say you wanna start running. Your cue could be laying out your running shoes the night before. When you see those shoes first thing in the morning, it triggers the routine of lacing up and hitting the pavement. And the reward? That rush of endorphins and the pride of crushing your run.

Now, how do you keep those positive habits going? It's all about taking baby steps. No need to flip your life upside down overnight—who's got the energy for that? Start with something easy. If you wanna drink more water, don't dive headfirst into chugging a gallon a day. Instead, fill a glass of water and plop it on your desk. Each time you sit down to work, take a sip. Before long, you'll be reaching for that glass without even thinkin' about it.

Here's a handy little list to guide you on your quest to build those healthy habits:

1. **Start small**: Pick one habit to focus on. Don't overwhelm yourself.

2. **Be consistent**: Try to do your new habit at the same time every day. This helps create that cue.

3. **Track your progress**: Use a journal or an app to see how you're doing. Celebrate those small wins!

4. **Find an accountability buddy**: Share your goals with a friend who can cheer you on and keep you in check.

5. **Be patient**: Remember, habits take time to form. If you slip up, don't beat yourself up. Just get back on track.

Now, let's chat about how habits can turbocharge your personal growth. Picture this: every time you engage in a positive habit, you're stacking the odds in your favor. It's like building a house. Each brick you lay—whether it's reading a book, exercising, or practicing gratitude—creates a solid foundation for your life.

When you consistently show up for yourself, you start to see some real changes. You become more confident, resilient, and ready to tackle whatever life throws your way. Those little habits? They add up to big transformations. You might find yourself feeling more energized, focused, and motivated to chase your dreams. It's like flipping a switch inside you that lights up your path forward.

But hey, don't just take my word for it. Think about someone you admire—maybe it's a friend, a mentor, or even a public figure. Chances are, they've built their success on a foundation of healthy habits. They didn't get there by chance. They showed up, day in and day out, making choices that aligned with their goals.

So, as you set off on this journey of building healthy habits, keep your eyes on the prize. Visualize where you wanna be and let that vision guide you. Every step you take is a step toward becoming the best version of yourself. And remember, you've got the power within you to make it happen.

In the end, it's not just about the habits themselves; it's about who you become in the process. Embrace the journey, celebrate your progress, and keep pushing forward. You've got this, and I believe in you! Now, go out there and start building those habits that'll change your life for the better. The world's waiting for your brilliance to shine!

Now, let's dig a bit deeper into why habits matter so much. Think of habits like the oil in a car engine. Without it, things grind to a halt. They keep everything running smoothly. When you've got good habits in place, you're setting yourself up for success. It's like having a roadmap for your life. You know where you're headed, and you've got the tools to get there.

Ever notice how some folks just seem to have it all together? They hit the gym regularly, eat healthy, and always seem to be in a good mood. That's no accident. They've built those habits over time. It's like they've created a recipe for success, and they keep adding ingredients until they get it just right.

And let's not forget about the power of community. Surrounding yourself with like-minded people can seriously boost your motivation. It's like being part of a team. You cheer each other on, share tips, and hold each other accountable. Plus, it's way more fun to tackle challenges with friends.

Think about it: when you're in a group, you're less likely to bail on your goals. You've got folks counting on you, and that can be a powerful motivator. So, find your tribe! Whether it's a running group, a book club, or a cooking class, get out there and connect with others who share your interests.

Now, let's talk about setbacks. Spoiler alert: they happen. Life's not a straight line, and sometimes you'll trip up. Maybe you skip a workout or eat that extra slice of cake. It happens to the best of us. The key is not to let it derail you. Dust yourself off and get back in the game. It's all part of the process.

Think of setbacks like a speed bump on the road. They might slow you down, but they don't have to stop you. Learn from them. What went wrong? How can you adjust your approach? Use those moments as stepping stones rather than stumbling blocks.

And here's a little secret: you don't have to be perfect. In fact, striving for perfection can be a total buzzkill. Instead, aim for progress. Celebrate the small victories along the way. Did you drink more water today than yesterday? Awesome! Did you go for a walk instead of binge-watching that show? High five! Every little win counts.

Let's also touch on the idea of self-compassion. It's easy to be hard on ourselves when we slip up. But what if, instead of beating yourself up, you treated yourself like a friend? Would you tell a buddy they're a failure for missing a workout? Nah! You'd encourage them to get back on track. So, practice that same kindness with yourself.

Now, here's where it gets interesting. As you build these healthy habits, you'll start to notice shifts in your mindset. You'll become more resilient, more adaptable. You'll start to see challenges as opportunities rather than roadblocks. It's like putting on a new pair of glasses—you see the world differently.

And guess what? That shift can have a ripple effect. When you feel good about yourself, you're more likely to spread that positivity to others. It's contagious! You'll inspire your friends, family, and coworkers to step up their game, too.

So, let's wrap this up with a little pep talk. You've got the power to create the life you want. It's not always easy, but it's worth it. Building healthy habits is like planting seeds. You nurture them, give them sunlight, and eventually, they grow into something beautiful.

Remember, every small step you take is a step in the right direction. You don't have to climb the mountain in one go. Just take it one step at a time. And when you stumble, laugh it off and keep going. Life's too short to sweat the small stuff.

So, what are you waiting for? Get out there and start building those habits that'll change your life for the better. The world's waiting for your brilliance to shine! You've got this!

Chapter 8

The Power of Gratitude

Gratitude, my friend, is like a secret superpower. It's that little spark that lights up your day, even when the clouds are hanging low. Imagine waking up each morning, your feet hitting the floor, and instead of diving into the chaos of your to-do list, you pause. You take a breath and think about one thing—just one—that you're thankful for. That simple act can shift your whole perspective. It's like putting on a fresh pair of glasses that lets you see the beauty in the ordinary.

Let's dive into the benefits of a gratitude practice. First off, it's been shown to improve your mental health. Studies have found that people who regularly practice gratitude report fewer symptoms of depression and anxiety. It's like a natural mood booster! When you focus on what you have instead of what you lack, your brain starts to rewire itself. You become more resilient, more optimistic. It's like planting seeds of positivity that blossom into a garden of joy.

But don't just take my word for it. Think about how you feel when someone expresses gratitude towards you. It lifts you up, doesn't it? Now, imagine turning that same energy inward. When you acknowledge your own blessings, it's like giving yourself a warm hug. You start to notice the little things—a kind smile from a stranger, the warmth of the sun on your face, or the comforting sound of rain tapping against your window. These moments, often overlooked, become treasures in your daily life.

Now, let's get practical. How do you cultivate this attitude of gratitude? Daily rituals can make all the difference. Start simple. Keep a gratitude journal. Each night, jot down three things you're grateful for. They can be big or small—like a delicious cup of coffee or a heartfelt conversation with a friend. The key is consistency. Make it a part of your routine, and soon enough, it'll feel like second nature.

Another great ritual is to share your gratitude with others. Send a quick text to a friend, letting them know how much they mean to you. Or, write a thank-you note to someone who's made a difference in your life. This not only boosts your mood but spreads positivity like wildfire. You'll be surprised how a simple message can brighten someone's day, and in turn, lift your spirits too.

And let's not forget about mindfulness. Incorporate gratitude into your mindfulness practice. When you meditate, focus on what you're thankful for. Feel it in your bones. Let that warmth wash over you. It's a beautiful way to ground yourself and connect with the present moment.

Now, let's sprinkle in some transformative stories. There's a tale about a woman named Emily. She was going through a rough patch—lost her job, feeling isolated, and battling negative thoughts. One day, a friend suggested she start a gratitude journal. Reluctantly, she gave it a shot. At first, it felt silly. But as the days went by, she began to notice the little things. A blooming flower in her garden, the laughter of children playing outside, the taste of her favorite meal. Each entry shifted her mindset, and slowly, she felt the weight of despair lift.

Then there's the story of a man named Joe. He was struggling with addiction and had hit rock bottom. In a moment of clarity, he decided to try gratitude as part of his recovery process. He started attending a support group where they shared what they were thankful for. At first, he felt out of place, but as he listened to others, he began to see the silver linings in his life. He realized he was grateful for his health, his family's support, and the chance to start anew. This practice became a cornerstone of his journey to sobriety, reminding him that even in the darkest times, there's always a glimmer of hope.

These stories remind us that gratitude isn't just a feel-good exercise; it's a transformative practice that can change lives. It can help you navigate through tough times and come out stronger on the other side.

So, as you embark on this journey of gratitude, remember that it's not about perfection. It's about progress. Celebrate the small wins, and don't be too hard on yourself if some days feel heavier than others. Each moment you choose gratitude is a step towards a brighter outlook.

Visualize your success. Picture yourself waking up each day, filled with appreciation. Imagine how that would ripple out into your life. You'd approach challenges with a lighter heart. You'd find joy in the mundane. You'd connect more deeply with those around you. That's the power of gratitude, my friend. It's like a warm blanket on a chilly night, wrapping you in comfort and reminding you that you're never alone.

So, take a moment right now. Think of one thing you're grateful for. Hold onto that feeling. Let it inspire you to cultivate gratitude in your daily life. You've got this! Embrace the journey, and watch how your world transforms.

Chapter 9

Nurturing Relationships

We all know that life can be a wild ride, filled with ups and downs, twists and turns. But here's the thing: you don't have to navigate it alone. The connections we forge with others can be like a sturdy bridge over turbulent waters, helping us grow and thrive in ways we might never have imagined. So let's dive into the magic of nurturing relationships and how they can fuel your personal growth journey.

Connection isn't just a nice-to-have; it's a must-have. Think of it like watering a plant. Without water, that little green sprout struggles to survive. It wilts, it droops, and it just doesn't reach its full potential. In the same way, when we lack connection, we can feel lost, disconnected, and unsure of ourselves. But when we cultivate meaningful relationships, we create an environment that fosters growth, encouragement, and support. It's like surrounding yourself with a team of cheerleaders, all rooting for you to succeed.

So how do we build these meaningful relationships? First off, it's about being intentional. You gotta put yourself out there. Start by engaging in activities that light you up—hobbies, classes, community events. When you're doing what you love, you're bound to meet folks who share your passions. And trust me, that common ground can be a powerful foundation for a lasting connection.

Next, don't shy away from vulnerability. I know, I know—being vulnerable can feel like standing on a tightrope. But let me tell you, it's in those moments of openness that real connections are formed. Share your dreams, your fears, and your experiences. When you let others see the real you, it creates an invitation for them to do the same. It's like opening the door to a warm, welcoming space where both of you can thrive.

Communication is another key ingredient. And I'm not just talking about chit-chat over coffee. I mean deep, meaningful conversations where you really listen and engage. Ask questions that spark thought and reflection. Show genuine interest in the other person's story. You'd be amazed at how much deeper your relationships can grow when you take the time to truly connect.

Now, let's talk about support. When you're on your journey of transformation, having a solid support system can make all the difference. Your relationships can provide encouragement during tough times and celebrate your victories, no matter how small. Think of them as your personal pit crew, ready to refuel you when you're running low on energy. When you face challenges, lean on your loved ones. Share your struggles and allow them to lift you up. Remember, it's not a sign of weakness; it's a testament to the strength of your connections.

But don't forget, nurturing relationships is a two-way street. It's not just about what you can get; it's about what you can give. Be there for others, offer your support, and show appreciation for their presence in your life. A simple "thank you" or a heartfelt note can go a long way in strengthening those bonds. It's the little things that often mean the most.

As you navigate this journey of building relationships, keep in mind that it's okay to let go of connections that no longer serve you. Sometimes, we hold onto relationships out of habit or obligation. But if they drain your energy or hinder your growth, it might be time to reassess. Surround yourself with those who uplift you, challenge you, and inspire you to be your best self.

Now, let's take a moment to visualize the impact of these nurturing relationships. Picture yourself surrounded by a circle of friends and loved ones, each one cheering you on, offering their wisdom, and sharing in your joys and sorrows. Imagine how that support can propel you forward, making your journey feel lighter and more fulfilling. This is the power of connection, and it's within your reach.

In closing, remember that nurturing relationships is not just about building a network; it's about creating a community of support, love, and encouragement. As you embark on this journey, be open to new connections, embrace vulnerability, and invest in the relationships that matter. Your growth is intertwined with those around you, and together, you can achieve incredible things.

So go on, my friend. Reach out, connect, and nurture those relationships. You've got this! And as you do, watch how your life transforms in ways you never thought possible. Your journey is just beginning, and the connections you make will be the fuel that propels you forward.

Chapter 10

Self-Care: More Than Just a Trend

Let's get real about self-care, folks. It's not just some fancy phrase people toss around on social media. Nah, it's a lifeline. In this crazy, chaotic world, taking care of yourself is crucial. It's about recognizing that you matter, that your needs deserve attention. Seriously, how often do we rush through life, juggling responsibilities, and forget to check in with ourselves? It's like driving on fumes—you can only go so far before you stall out.

So, what's self-care all about? It comes in many flavors, and it's essential to find what clicks for you. Think of it like a buffet—you've got choices galore. There's physical self-care, which includes stuff like working out, eating right, and getting enough shut-eye. Then there's emotional self-care, which might involve journaling, chatting with a friend, or curling up with a book that makes you feel all warm and fuzzy inside. Don't overlook social self-care, either! That's all about connecting with those who lift you up. And let's not forget spiritual self-care, which could be meditation, yoga, or just soaking in the beauty of nature.

The cool thing about self-care? It's super personal. What fills your tank might leave someone else running on empty. So, take the time to explore what self-care means for you. It could be as chill as soaking in a bubble bath or as adventurous as climbing a mountain. Whatever it is, own it!

Let me tell you a little story. I've got this friend, let's call her Lisa. She was the ultimate caretaker—always there for everyone, dishing out advice, and planning get-togethers. But one day, she hit a wall. Burnout knocked on her door, and she realized she couldn't keep pouring from an empty cup. So, she decided to switch things up and signed up for a pottery class.

Now, Lisa never thought of herself as an artist, but she figured, "Why not?"

At first, she was all thumbs with the clay. But as the sessions rolled on, she found herself getting lost in the process. The spinning wheel became her sanctuary—a place where her mind could chill, and her soul could breathe. Over time, she crafted some beautiful pieces, but more importantly, she built a new relationship with herself. That pottery class turned into a weekly ritual, a promise to prioritize her self-care. It was a game-changer. Lisa learned that taking time for yourself isn't selfish; it's downright essential.

Now, I can hear you thinking, "But I don't have time for self-care!" Oh, I get it. Life's a whirlwind. But here's the kicker: self-care doesn't have to be a grand event. It can be tiny, manageable moments sprinkled throughout your day. Maybe it's enjoying your morning coffee in peace before the chaos kicks in. Or taking five minutes to stretch and breathe deeply. Even a quick stroll around the block can do wonders.

Think of self-care as little investments in yourself. Each moment you carve out for your well-being is like depositing a bit of joy into your emotional bank account. And trust me, when that account starts to fill up, you'll find more energy, patience, and resilience to tackle whatever life throws your way.

Let's dive deeper into the different flavors of self-care. Physical self-care is a biggie. Regular exercise, eating nourishing foods, and getting enough sleep are foundational. When your body feels good, your mind usually follows suit. So whether it's a brisk walk, a yoga session, or dancing like nobody's watching in your living room, get moving!

Emotional self-care is just as crucial. This might mean setting boundaries—saying no when you need to or carving out time for activities that spark joy. Don't underestimate the power of a good cry or a hearty laugh. Journaling can also be a fantastic outlet, helping you process your thoughts and feelings.

And let's not forget social self-care. Surround yourself with people who lift you up, make you laugh, and support your dreams. It's about creating a community that feels like home. And if you find yourself in toxic relationships, it's okay to step back. Protect your peace, my friend.

Spiritual self-care looks different for everyone. It might involve meditation, prayer, or simply soaking up nature's beauty. For some, it's about finding a sense of purpose or connection to something greater than themselves. Whatever it is, nurture that aspect of your life.

As you explore these different forms of self-care, listen to your heart. What feels right for you? What brings you joy? Dive into those activities with an open mind and heart.

Back to Lisa for a sec. After her pottery journey, she felt a shift. She was more present, patient, and in tune with herself. She even started advocating for self-care—not just for herself but for her friends, too. She organized a monthly "self-care night" where they'd try different activities together—painting, cooking, or even binge-watching their favorite shows. It became a beautiful way to connect, support each other, and remind one another of the importance of taking a break.

Self-care isn't a one-and-done deal. It's an ongoing journey, a commitment to yourself. Just like any journey, there'll be bumps along the way. Some days, you'll feel like you're on top of the world; other days, well, you might feel like you've hit a wall. That's totally okay! It's all part of the process.

Here's the real deal: self-care isn't a luxury; it's a necessity. When you prioritize your well-being, you're not just benefiting yourself—you're benefiting everyone around you. A well-cared-for you is a gift to the world. You'll be more equipped to handle challenges, support others, and pursue your passions.

So, as you dive into this self-care journey, visualize it. Picture yourself thriving, feeling energized, and embracing life with open arms. Imagine the ripple effect your self-care will have—not just on you but on your family, friends, and community.

Take a moment to reflect on your own self-care practices. What's working? What could use a little tweak? And if you haven't carved out time for yourself lately, I urge you to start today. Whether it's a five-minute break to breathe deeply or planning a fun outing for yourself, take that step.

Remember, you're worthy of care, love, and attention. You've got the power within you to transform your life through self-care. So go on, embrace it! Your journey awaits, and I can't wait to see how you bloom.

Let's talk about some practical self-care strategies. First off, how about creating a self-care routine? You don't need to go overboard—just a few simple things you can do daily or weekly. Maybe it's a morning ritual that includes a cup of tea and some quiet time. Or a nightly routine where you disconnect from screens and dive into a good book.

And hey, don't forget about the power of movement. It doesn't have to be a full-blown workout. A little stretching, a dance party in your living room, or even just a brisk walk can do wonders for your mood. It's all about finding what feels good for you.

Let's also chat about mindfulness. Taking a few moments each day to check in with yourself can be a game-changer. Whether it's through meditation, deep breathing, or simply sitting in silence, being present can help you reconnect with your thoughts and feelings.

And what about creativity? Engaging in creative activities can be a fantastic way to unwind. Whether it's painting, writing, or even cooking, letting your creative juices flow can bring a sense of joy and fulfillment. Plus, it's a great way to express yourself!

Now, let's not ignore the importance of rest. Seriously, rest is not a sign of weakness; it's a vital part of self-care. Allow yourself to take breaks, whether it's a power nap or just some downtime on the couch. Your body and mind will thank you.

Social connections are key, too. Make it a point to reach out to friends or family. Schedule regular catch-ups, whether it's a coffee date or a virtual hangout. Surrounding yourself with supportive people can boost your mood and remind you that you're not alone in this journey.

And if you're feeling overwhelmed, don't hesitate to seek help. Talking to a therapist or counselor can provide valuable support and guidance. There's no shame in asking for help when you need it.

Now, let's circle back to the idea of self-care being a journey. It's not about perfection; it's about progress. Some days, you'll nail it, and other days, you might drop the ball. That's life! The key is to keep showing up for yourself, no matter what.

Remember, self-care is a lifelong commitment. It's not a sprint; it's a marathon. So, pace yourself and be gentle with yourself along the way. Celebrate your victories, no matter how small, and learn from the challenges you face.

As you embark on this self-care journey, keep your eyes on the prize. You're not just doing this for yourself; you're doing it for the people you love, too. When you take care of yourself, you're better equipped to show up for others. You become a source of strength and support, and that's pretty powerful.

So, let's wrap this up. Self-care is essential, my friend. It's not just a trend; it's a necessity. You're worthy of love, care, and attention. Take the time to explore what self-care looks like for you, and don't be afraid to embrace it. Your journey is waiting, and I can't wait to see how you thrive. Now, go out there and bloom!

Chapter 11

Harnessing the Power of Affirmations

Affirmations, my friend, are like the little whispers of encouragement we all need from time to time. They're powerful tools that can shape our thoughts, influence our actions, and ultimately transform our lives. Imagine standing in front of a mirror, looking deep into your own eyes, and declaring, "I am worthy. I am capable. I am enough." Feels good, doesn't it? That's the magic of affirmations. They're not just words; they're declarations that can shift your mindset and set the stage for success.

Understanding the impact of affirmations is the first step in harnessing their power. You see, our minds are like fertile soil, and what we plant in them grows. If you're constantly feeding yourself negative thoughts, that's what's gonna sprout. But when you plant positive affirmations, you're nurturing a garden of possibilities. Research shows that affirmations can help reduce stress, boost self-esteem, and even improve overall well-being. It's like giving your brain a little pep talk, reminding it of all the good stuff that's already inside you.

Now, let's talk about creating personalized affirmations for success. This is where the real fun begins! You want your affirmations to resonate with you on a deep level. So grab a pen and paper, and let's get to work. Start by asking yourself: What do I want to achieve? What limiting beliefs am I holding onto? Once you've got that clarity, craft affirmations that speak directly to those desires and challenges. For instance, if you struggle with self-doubt, you might say, "I trust myself to make the right decisions." If you're aiming for a promotion at work, try something like, "I am a valuable asset to my team and deserve success." Make 'em specific, make 'em personal, and make 'em feel true.

But don't stop there. To really make these affirmations stick, you've gotta integrate them into your daily routine. Say them out loud in the morning while you brush your teeth, write them in your journal, or even post them on sticky notes around your house. The more you repeat them, the more they become a part of your inner dialogue. It's like training a muscle—consistency is key. You're building a new narrative for your life, one that aligns with your dreams and aspirations.

Now, let's sprinkle in some real-life examples of affirmations in action. You might be surprised to learn that some of the most successful people in the world swear by this practice. Take Oprah Winfrey, for instance. She's often talked about how affirmations helped her overcome a tumultuous childhood and achieve her dreams. By repeating affirmations like "I am worthy of love and success," she reprogrammed her mind to embrace positivity and possibility. And look where that got her!

Another inspiring story comes from the world of sports. Michael Phelps, the legendary swimmer, is known for his intense mental preparation. Before each race, he would visualize his success and repeat affirmations to himself, reinforcing his belief in his abilities. Those affirmations fueled his confidence and propelled him to become the most decorated Olympian of all time. Talk about a powerful testament to the impact of positive thinking!

But let's not just look at the celebrities; let's bring it back to you. Think about a time when you faced a challenge—maybe it was a tough job interview or a presentation that had you sweating bullets. What if, before that moment, you had taken a few minutes to repeat affirmations that reminded you of your skills and strengths? Imagine how that could've shifted your mindset and boosted your confidence. That's the beauty of affirmations—they empower you to take charge of your thoughts and actions.

As you embark on this journey of harnessing the power of affirmations, remember that it's not about perfection. It's about progress. You're gonna have days when you doubt yourself, and that's okay. The key is to acknowledge those feelings without letting them define you. When those negative thoughts creep in, counter them with your affirmations. "I am resilient. I can handle whatever comes my way." It's like putting on armor against the negativity that tries to drag you down.

And here's a little secret: you don't have to do this alone. Share your affirmations with friends or family. Create a support system where you can uplift each other. You might even inspire someone else to start their own affirmation practice. Together, you can build a community of positivity and encouragement, and that's a beautiful thing.

So, my friend, as you dive into the world of affirmations, keep this in mind: you have the power to transform your mind and, in turn, transform your life. It's all about believing in yourself and embracing the journey. Each affirmation is a step toward the life you desire, and every time you repeat them, you're reinforcing your worth and potential.

Now, let's wrap this up with a little action plan. Grab that pen and paper, and start jotting down your affirmations. Make them personal, make them powerful, and most importantly, make them yours. Set a reminder on your phone to say them daily, and watch how your mindset begins to shift. Celebrate the small wins along the way, because every step counts.

You got this! Embrace the power within you, and let your affirmations guide you toward a brighter, more fulfilling life.

Remember, it's not just about the destination; it's about the journey and the person you become along the way. Now go on, get out there, and start affirming your greatness!

Chapter 12

Embracing Vulnerability

Vulnerability. Man, that word can make people fidget, right? But here's the kicker: there's some serious strength hidden in being vulnerable. It's like panning for gold in a muddy creek—you gotta sift through the muck to find those shiny nuggets. When you let your guard down, you're not just opening up; you're unlocking a whole new level of authenticity, connection, and personal growth. It's not about putting your heart on display for everyone to see. Nah, it's about being real, being human, and accepting the messy parts of life.

Think about it for a sec. When you drop your defenses, you're inviting others in. You create a vibe where real talk can happen—where you can spill your guts about your struggles and celebrate your wins. It's like a dance; you take a step forward, and the other person does too. That's how you build bonds, deepen friendships, and let love blossom.

So, how do you dive into this whole vulnerability thing? Honestly, it's not as scary as it sounds. Here's a few ways to help you open up and connect with folks:

First off, share your story. Start small, okay? Maybe talk about a tough breakup or a job you lost. When you share, you give others the green light to do the same. It's like lighting a candle in a dark room—everything feels warmer.

Next up, ask open-ended questions. Ditch the boring "How are you?" and switch it up with "What's been on your mind lately?" or "What's a challenge you've faced recently?" These kinds of questions get people talking and show you actually care about their experiences.

Then, there's active listening. When someone spills their guts to you, listen with your whole heart. Nod, make eye contact, and don't rush to jump in with your own story. Sometimes, just being there and really hearing someone is the most powerful gift you can give.

And hey, don't be afraid to be honest about your feelings. It's totally cool to say, "I'm feeling a bit overwhelmed" or "I'm scared about what's next." Being real breeds trust. When you open up about how you feel, it encourages others to do the same. It's like throwing a pebble in a pond—those ripples spread out, creating a wave of openness.

Lastly, celebrate imperfection. Let's be real—nobody's perfect. Share your quirks, your flops, and those moments that didn't go as planned. This makes you relatable and gives others the freedom to be imperfect too.

Now, let's dig into some stories that really show the beauty of growth through vulnerability.

Take Lisa, for instance. I met her at a workshop, and she was a real firecracker—always lighting up the room. But beneath that bubbly exterior, she was wrestling with anxiety. One day, she decided to share her story during a group session. The room went silent as she opened up about her battles with self-doubt and how it had held her back from chasing her dreams.

To her surprise, the moment she let it out, others started sharing their own struggles. It was like a dam bursting—everyone had been holding back, waiting for someone to take the plunge. By the end of that session, Lisa felt lighter and found a support system she never knew she needed.

Then there's Mark. He was the strong, silent type—the guy everyone turned to for advice, but he never let anyone see his own struggles. One day, after a rough week, he broke down and shared his feelings with a close friend. That simple act of vulnerability led to a heart-to-heart that changed their friendship.

Mark learned that being vulnerable didn't make him weak; it made him human. He discovered true strength lies in connecting with others on a deeper level. From that day on, he made it a point to be more open with his feelings, and guess what? He found a richer, more fulfilling life.

These stories show us that vulnerability isn't a weakness; it's a brave act of self-acceptance. When we embrace our vulnerabilities, we give others the freedom to do the same. It's this beautiful cycle of connection and growth.

As you navigate your own journey, keep this in mind: vulnerability is a superpower. It lets you connect with others in ways you never thought possible. It's the bridge to understanding, compassion, and love.

I get it—sometimes it feels scary, like standing on the edge of a cliff, peering into the unknown. But trust me, taking that leap is worth it. The connections you'll make and the growth you'll experience will turn every moment of uncertainty into a stepping stone toward something greater.

Take a moment to picture what embracing vulnerability could look like in your life. Imagine yourself sharing your story, connecting with others, and feeling that warm glow of acceptance wash over you. That's the magic of vulnerability. It's an invitation to live life fully, to show up as your true self, and to inspire others to do the same.

So go ahead, take that leap. Open your heart, share your truth, and watch as the world around you transforms. You've got this, my friend. Embrace the power within you, and let vulnerability be your guiding light.

Now, let's get real for a minute. We all have our moments of doubt. We've all been there, right? You know, those times when you feel like you're standing in front of a mirror, and all you see are your flaws. I mean, who hasn't had that moment of self-reflection where you just wanna crawl under a rock? But here's the thing: those moments of doubt? They're part of the human experience. And guess what? They don't define you.

I remember a time when I was grappling with my own vulnerability. I was at a party, and everyone was mingling, laughing, and sharing stories. I felt like an outsider looking in. I wanted to join the conversation, but that nagging voice in my head kept telling me, "What if they don't like you?" or "What if you say something dumb?" So, I stood there, sipping my drink, feeling like a wallflower.

But then, something shifted. I saw a guy across the room who looked just as lost as I felt. I took a deep breath, walked over, and said, "Hey, do you wanna grab a drink? I'm feeling kinda out of place." To my surprise, he laughed and said he felt the same way. That simple moment of vulnerability opened up a whole new conversation, and we ended up chatting for hours. It was a reminder that everyone has their insecurities, and sometimes, all it takes is one person to take that leap.

Now, let's talk about social media for a sec. It's a double-edged sword, right? On one hand, it connects us, and on the other, it can make us feel like we're living in a highlight reel. You scroll through Instagram, and it's all perfect selfies and exotic vacations. But here's the truth: those posts don't show the whole picture. They don't capture the late-night tears, the messy rooms, or the moments of doubt.

When we share our real lives—the good, the bad, and the ugly—we create a space for others to do the same. It's like saying, "Hey, I'm not perfect, and that's okay." It's refreshing, it's human, and it fosters connection. So, next time you're tempted to post a perfectly curated photo, consider sharing something a bit more real. You might just inspire someone else to do the same.

And let's not forget about the power of community. Surrounding yourself with people who get it can make all the difference. I once joined a support group, thinking it'd be a bunch of sad faces sharing their woes. But what I found was a group of incredible individuals who were all on their own journeys. We shared our stories, laughed at our mishaps, and lifted each other up. It was a reminder that vulnerability doesn't have to be a solo journey. It's way more powerful when you have a crew cheering you on.

You know what else is cool? Vulnerability can be a catalyst for change. When you own your story, you give others permission to do the same. It's like a ripple effect. Think about activists or leaders who share their personal experiences to drive change. They're not just talking the talk; they're walking the walk. They're showing us that embracing vulnerability can spark movements, inspire others, and create a sense of community.

Now, I get it—some folks might still be on the fence about this whole vulnerability thing. "Why should I expose myself?" they might ask. Well, here's the deal: by being vulnerable, you're not just helping yourself; you're also paving the way for others. You're creating a culture where it's okay to be human. And isn't that what we all want? A little more humanity in this crazy world?

So, here's my challenge to you: take a moment to reflect on your own life. Where can you embrace vulnerability? Maybe it's in a conversation with a friend, sharing a story at work, or even posting something real on social media. Whatever it is, lean into it. It might feel uncomfortable at first, but that's where the magic happens.

You might just find that vulnerability leads to deeper connections, more meaningful conversations, and a richer life. And who knows? You might inspire someone else to take that leap too.

Remember, vulnerability is not about being weak; it's about being brave enough to show up as your true self. It's about breaking down those walls and letting others in. So go on, embrace it. Let it be your guiding light. You've got this, and the world is waiting for you to shine.

In the end, vulnerability is a journey, not a destination. It's about progress, not perfection. So, take it one step at a time. Celebrate the little wins, and don't be too hard on yourself. We're all just trying to figure this thing called life out, and there's no right or wrong way to do it.

So, what do you say? Are you ready to take that leap? To embrace vulnerability and let it transform your life? I promise you won't regret it. It's a wild ride, but it's one worth taking. Open your heart, share your truth, and watch as the world around you shifts. You're not alone in this. We're all in it together, and there's so much beauty waiting on the other side of vulnerability.

Let's go out there and embrace it!

Chapter 13

The Role of Passion and Purpose

Finding your passion is like stumbling upon a hidden treasure chest in your own backyard. It's there, just waiting for you to dig a little deeper. So, let's roll up our sleeves and get to work. What gets your heart racing? What makes you lose track of time? Maybe it's painting, teaching, or helping others. Whatever it is, you gotta take the time to discover what truly ignites that fire within you.

Start by asking yourself some questions. What activities make you feel alive? When do you feel most fulfilled? Grab a notebook, and jot down your thoughts. This is your personal exploration, and there are no wrong answers here. Think back to your childhood—what did you love to do back then? Sometimes, the seeds of our passions are planted early in life, just waiting for the right moment to bloom.

Now, aligning your life with your purpose is where the magic happens. It's like tuning a guitar; you gotta make sure everything is in harmony. Once you've uncovered your passion, it's time to weave it into the fabric of your daily life. This means making choices that reflect your true self. Maybe it's changing careers, starting a side hustle, or even volunteering in your community. Whatever it is, don't be afraid to take those steps.

You see, when your life is aligned with your purpose, you'll find that everything flows more smoothly. It's like catching a wave while surfing; you ride it with ease and joy. And here's the kicker—when you're living your purpose, you become a magnet for motivation and fulfillment. Passion is the fuel that powers your journey.

Think of it this way: when you're passionate about something, it's like you've got a superpower. You wake up excited, ready to tackle the day. You're driven, and obstacles that once seemed insurmountable now feel like mere bumps in the road. That's the beauty of passion—it transforms challenges into stepping stones.

Let's talk about motivation for a second. You know those days when you just can't seem to get off the couch? When you're feeling like a lump on a log? Well, when you're fueled by passion, those days become rare. You'll find that motivation flows naturally. You'll be inspired to take action, to create, to connect. And when you do, fulfillment follows.

Imagine waking up every morning with a sense of purpose that propels you out of bed. You're not just going through the motions; you're living with intention. That's what passion does for you. It adds color to your life, like a vibrant painting splashed across a dull canvas.

But hey, let's keep it real. Discovering your passion and aligning it with your purpose isn't always a walk in the park. There might be times when you feel lost or unsure. That's okay! It's all part of the journey. Embrace those moments of uncertainty, because they often lead to the biggest breakthroughs.

You might find yourself at a crossroads, wondering which path to take. In those moments, trust your gut. Your intuition is a powerful guide. Listen to it. It knows what you need, even when your mind is filled with doubt.

As you explore your passions, don't be afraid to experiment. Try new things, take classes, or join groups that resonate with you. Each experience will teach you something valuable, even if it's just confirming what you don't want.

And remember, it's not about perfection. It's about progress. Celebrate the small wins along the way. Each step you take toward aligning your life with your purpose is a victory worth acknowledging.

Now, let's talk about the impact your passion can have on others. When you're living authentically, it inspires those around you. Your energy is contagious! People are drawn to your enthusiasm, and before you know it, you're not just transforming your own life—you're influencing others to do the same.

Picture this: you're at a gathering, sharing your passion with friends. Their eyes light up as they listen to your stories. You can see the spark of inspiration igniting within them. That's the power of passion—it's not just a personal journey; it's a ripple effect that can change lives.

So, let's wrap this up with a little exercise. Take a moment to visualize your life filled with passion and purpose. Picture yourself doing what you love, surrounded by people who uplift and support you. Feel the joy radiating from within. This is your potential. This is what you're capable of achieving.

Now, go out there and take action. Start small, but start somewhere. Whether it's dedicating a few hours a week to your passion or having a heart-to-heart with someone about your dreams, every step counts. You've got the power within you to transform your mind and, in turn, transform your life. Embrace it!

Remember, the journey of discovering your passion and aligning it with your purpose is ongoing. It's not a one-time event; it's a beautiful, ever-evolving process. Keep your heart open, stay curious, and let your passion lead the way. You're on the path to something incredible, and I can't wait to see where it takes you!

Chapter 14

Resilience in the Face of Failure

Failure. That word can slam into you like a freight train, right? But hold up—don't let it knock you down for good. It's not the end of your journey. Nah, it's just a little bump in the road, a pit stop on your way to wherever you're headed. Picture this: when you're learning to ride a bike, you're bound to wipe out. Scraped knees, bruised ego, you name it. But every time you hop back on, you're not just figuring out how to balance—you're toughening up. That's the magic ingredient.

Seeing failure as a stepping stone is crucial for flipping those setbacks into setups for something better. Seriously, failure isn't the bad guy in your story; it's more like that wise old friend who dishes out advice you didn't even know you needed. You know the saying: "Fall down seven times, get up eight." Each fall? It's a chance to learn something fresh about yourself, your ambitions, and the world around you.

Let's break it down a bit. How do you bounce back from those gut punches life throws at you? First, allow yourself to feel that disappointment. It's totally fine to be bummed out, to feel that sting deep down. But don't wallow in it forever. Shake it off and ask yourself, "What can I take away from this?" That simple shift in mindset can turn your defeat into a growth opportunity.

Now, let's talk about reframing your thoughts. Instead of saying, "I failed," flip it to "I learned." That little change can totally revamp your outlook. It's like trading in an old, rusty toolbox for a slick new one. You're arming yourself with the right tools to handle whatever life throws your way next.

Another nifty trick is setting small, doable goals. When you're facing a setback, it can feel like you're staring up at a mountain, overwhelmed by the peak. So, break it down! Focus on one step at a time. Celebrate those mini victories. Maybe it's jotting down a page in your journal, making that phone call you've been putting off, or just managing to get out of bed on a rough day. Each small win is like a building block, strengthening your resilience.

Now, let's sprinkle in some inspiration. Ever heard of J.K. Rowling? Before she was a household name, she got shot down by twelve publishers. Can you even wrap your head around that? But she didn't throw in the towel. Nope, she kept going, kept believing in her story. And look where that led her—millions of readers and a legacy that inspires folks to this day. That's resilience in full swing.

Or how about Thomas Edison? The guy famously said, "I have not failed. I've just found 10,000 ways that won't work." Seriously, 10,000! That's a whole lot of trial and error. But each failure brought him one step closer to inventing the light bulb. He didn't just bounce back; he bounced forward.

So, when you find yourself deep in the trenches of failure, remember these stories. They're not just tales of success; they're blueprints for resilience. You've got that same power within you.

As you navigate your own path, keep these strategies handy. Embrace the lessons failure throws your way. Reframe your thoughts. Set those small goals and give yourself a pat on the back for your progress. And when the urge to quit creeps in, think of those who've walked this road before you.

In the end, resilience isn't just about bouncing back. It's about rising stronger, wiser, and ready to tackle whatever comes next. You're not just surviving; you're thriving. And that, my friend, is the true power within you. So go on, embrace your failures, learn from them, and let them propel you to greatness. You got this!

Let's dig a little deeper into what resilience really means. It's not just a buzzword; it's a way of life. Think about it— life's gonna throw curveballs. You can't avoid them. But how you react? That's what counts. It's like a game of dodgeball. You can either duck and cover or get hit and learn how to dodge better next time.

Take a moment to reflect on your own experiences. Have you ever faced a setback that felt insurmountable? Maybe it was a job loss, a failed relationship, or a missed opportunity. In those moments, it's easy to feel like the world's crumbling around you. But if you take a step back, you might find that those tough times shaped you in ways you never expected.

For example, let's say you applied for your dream job and didn't get it. Ouch, right? But think about what you learned through the process. Maybe you honed your interview skills, or perhaps you realized that the job wasn't actually the right fit for you. Each disappointment can lead to self-discovery, and that's where the real growth happens.

But hey, let's not sugarcoat it. Sometimes, failure can feel like a punch to the gut. It can shake your confidence and make you question everything. And that's totally normal. We're human, after all. But here's the kicker: it's how you respond that defines you. You can either let it break you or use it as fuel to rise higher.

Now, let's chat about the importance of community. Surrounding yourself with supportive folks can make all the difference. When you're down in the dumps, having a friend to lean on or a mentor to guide you can be a game-changer. They can offer fresh perspectives, share their own stories of resilience, and remind you that you're not alone in this.

Think about it—who do you turn to when times get tough? Maybe it's a family member, a best friend, or even a coworker. Those connections are vital. They can help you see the light at the end of the tunnel when you're stuck in the dark. And let's be real, sometimes you just need someone to say, "Hey, it's okay to feel this way. You'll get through it."

But don't just rely on others. Cultivating self-compassion is key. Treat yourself with kindness when things go south. Instead of beating yourself up, give yourself a break. It's okay to be imperfect. Remember, even the most successful people have their off days. You're not alone in this struggle.

And while we're on the topic of self-compassion, let's not forget the power of humor. Laughter can be a fantastic antidote to failure. When you can laugh at yourself, it lightens the load. It's like saying, "Yeah, I messed up, but that's just part of the ride." Embracing the lighter side of things can help you gain perspective and move forward.

Now, let's pivot a bit and talk about the role of mindfulness. Being present in the moment can help you process failure more effectively. Instead of getting lost in negative thoughts or worrying about the future, try grounding yourself. Take a deep breath, acknowledge your feelings, and then focus on what you can control. Mindfulness helps you stay centered and can be a powerful tool for resilience.

And speaking of tools, let's explore some practical techniques. Journaling can be a fantastic outlet for processing your emotions. Write down your thoughts, your fears, and what you've learned from your failures. It's like having a heart-to-heart with yourself. Plus, looking back on your entries can remind you of how far you've come.

Another technique is visualization. Picture yourself overcoming obstacles. Imagine what success looks like for you. Visualization can help you build confidence and reinforce your belief in your ability to bounce back.

Now, let's not forget the importance of self-reflection. After a setback, take some time to analyze what went wrong. Was it a lack of preparation? Did you let fear hold you back? Understanding the root cause can help you avoid similar pitfalls in the future. It's all about learning from your experiences.

And here's a thought: don't be afraid to ask for help. Whether it's seeking advice from a mentor or talking to a therapist, reaching out can provide you with valuable insights. There's no shame in leaning on others when you need support.

As we wrap this up, remember that resilience is a journey, not a destination. You're not gonna master it overnight. It takes time, practice, and a whole lot of self-love. Embrace the ups and downs. Celebrate your progress, no matter how small. Each step forward is a victory.

So, when life throws you a curveball, don't forget these strategies. Embrace failure as a teacher. Reframe your thoughts. Set those bite-sized goals. Lean on your community. Cultivate self-compassion and humor. Practice mindfulness and self-reflection. And most importantly, keep pushing forward.

In the grand scheme of things, resilience is about more than just bouncing back. It's about rising stronger, wiser, and ready to tackle whatever life throws your way. You're not just surviving; you're thriving. And that, my friend, is the true power within you. So go on, embrace your failures, learn from them, and let them propel you to greatness. You got this!

Chapter 15

Celebrating Your Journey

Let's talk about reflection. Seriously, it's one of those things we often overlook while we're hustling through life. But here's the deal: taking a moment to look back can be like flipping on a light switch in a dark room. It's not just about where you end up; it's about every twist and turn along the way—the bumps, the wins, and yeah, even those faceplants. When you stop to reflect, you start to see the strength you've built up over time. You recognize the resilience that's been woven into your experiences. And that's something to celebrate, my friend.

But hey, don't just take my word for it. Think about it like this: when you take time to celebrate your journey, you're not just giving yourself a pat on the back; you're laying down a solid foundation for future wins. Every little step you take, even the tiniest ones, is a piece of the bigger puzzle that makes up your life story. So, let's dive into some cool ways to help you acknowledge how far you've come.

First off, let's chat about journaling. It's like a magic trick for your brain! Grab a notebook and start scribbling down your thoughts, feelings, and experiences. Reflect on your day, your week, or even your month. What went right? What challenges did you tackle? How'd you get through 'em? When you write it down, it becomes real. You can actually see the progress you've made, and it's way easier to appreciate the journey. Plus, there's something super freeing about putting pen to paper. It's like letting go of a balloon; you watch it float away, and you feel lighter.

Next up, let's get creative with a "win wall." Sounds fun, right? Find a corkboard or a spot on your wall and start pinning up your achievements—big or small. Maybe it's a compliment from a friend, a goal you crushed, or even a personal milestone. Every time you glance at that wall, you're reminded of how far you've come. It's like a visual celebration of your journey, a little boost when things get tough.

And don't sleep on gratitude! Take a moment each day to think about what you're thankful for. It can be as simple as a hot cup of coffee or a smile from a stranger. When you focus on the good stuff, it shifts your mindset. You start seeing the beauty in your journey, which makes the rough patches feel a bit less overwhelming.

Here's a little secret: celebrating small wins can snowball into bigger successes. It's like planting seeds in a garden. You water them, care for them, and before you know it, you've got a beautiful bloom. When you acknowledge those small victories, you're fueling your motivation. You're saying, "Hey, look what I've done!" And that momentum? It builds. It grows.

Picture this: when you celebrate a small win, you're creating a positive feedback loop. Your brain releases those feel-good chemicals, and suddenly, you're pumped to tackle the next challenge. It's like a snowball rolling down a hill, picking up speed and size. Each small win becomes a stepping stone to bigger and better things.

Let's take a moment to imagine your future. Picture yourself crossing the finish line of a marathon. You've trained hard, faced setbacks, and pushed through the pain. As you cross that line, it's not just relief you feel; it's an overwhelming sense of pride. That's what celebrating your journey is all about. It's about recognizing every single step that got you there.

So, how do you keep this celebration going? Make it a habit. Set aside time each week to reflect on your progress. Maybe it's Sunday evening with a cup of tea, or a Friday morning ritual to kick off the weekend. Whatever it is, make it a priority. Treat it like an appointment you can't miss.

And here's a fun idea: celebrate with others! Share your wins with friends or family. Create a little accountability group where you can lift each other up and celebrate each other's journeys. It's like having your own cheerleading squad. Who doesn't love a little extra support?

Every journey's unique. What works for one person might not work for another, and that's totally cool. The key is to find what resonates with you. Try out different techniques, and don't be afraid to get creative.

As you navigate your journey, remember: it's not just about the big milestones. It's about the everyday moments that shape you. Celebrate the small victories, the lessons learned, and the growth you experience along the way. Each moment is like a brushstroke on the canvas of your life, creating a masterpiece that tells your story.

So here's your challenge: take a moment today to reflect on your journey. What have you accomplished? What challenges have you overcome? Write it down, create your win wall, or share it with someone who supports you.

You've got this! Embrace the power of celebration. Let it fuel your fire and propel you forward. Because when you celebrate your journey, you're not just recognizing where you've been; you're paving the way for where you're going.

And let me tell ya, the road ahead is bright. You're capable of incredible things, and each step you take is a testament to your strength and resilience. So go on, celebrate! You deserve it.

Now, let's get into some real talk about why this whole celebration thing matters. You see, life can be a wild ride. One minute you're on top of the world, and the next, you're facing a mountain of challenges. But when you take the time to celebrate your journey, you're not just looking back; you're also setting the stage for what's next. It's like putting on your favorite playlist before heading out for a night on the town—it gets you in the right mindset!

Think about it: how often do we get so caught up in chasing the next big thing that we forget to appreciate what we've already accomplished? It's like running a race and never stopping to catch your breath. Sure, you want to finish strong, but you also need to recognize the effort it took to get there.

And let's be real—life's tough. We all face setbacks, disappointments, and moments when we feel like giving up. But when you celebrate your journey, you're reminding yourself of the strength you've shown in overcoming those hurdles. You're building a mental bank of victories that you can draw on when the going gets tough. It's like having a secret stash of confidence ready to go when you need it most.

Now, I know some folks might think, "Why bother celebrating? It's just a small win." But here's the kicker: those small wins? They add up. They're the building blocks of your success. Think of them as stepping stones across a river. Each one gets you closer to the other side, and before you know it, you've crossed over to a whole new level of achievement.

Let's get a bit personal here. I remember a time when I was struggling to hit a goal. I felt like I was running in circles, and nothing seemed to work. But then I started celebrating the little things—like getting out of bed on time or finishing a task I'd been putting off. Those tiny victories shifted my perspective. Suddenly, I wasn't just focused on the big goal; I was recognizing the progress I was making along the way. And that made all the difference.

So, how can you incorporate celebration into your daily life? It doesn't have to be a grand event. It can be as simple as treating yourself to your favorite snack after a long day or taking a moment to enjoy a sunset. The key is to make it intentional. Set aside time to acknowledge your wins, no matter how small.

You could even create a "celebration jar." Grab a jar and some slips of paper. Whenever you achieve something—big or small—write it down and toss it in the jar. At the end of the month or year, you can read through all those little victories. It's a great way to remind yourself of how far you've come.

And let's not forget about the power of storytelling. Share your journey with others. Talk about your challenges, your wins, and everything in between. When you share your story, you not only celebrate your journey but also inspire others to reflect on theirs. It's like passing the torch, lighting up the path for someone else.

Now, if you're thinking, "But I'm not where I want to be yet," that's okay! Celebrating your journey doesn't mean you have to be at the finish line. It's about acknowledging the progress you've made, no matter how small. Every step counts, and each one is a part of your unique story.

Let's be honest: life's a journey, not a destination. We hear that all the time, but it's so true. Embrace the ups and downs, the twists and turns. Celebrate the moments that make you laugh, the lessons that teach you, and the challenges that shape you. Each experience is a brushstroke on your life's canvas, creating a beautiful masterpiece that tells your story.

So, what are you waiting for? Start celebrating today! Reflect on your journey, acknowledge your wins, and share your story with others. You've got this! Embrace the power of celebration. Let it fuel your fire and propel you forward. Because when you celebrate your journey, you're not just recognizing where you've been; you're paving the way for where you're going.

And trust me, the road ahead is full of potential. You're capable of amazing things, and every step you take is a testament to your strength and resilience. So go on, celebrate! You deserve it. You've earned it. Now get out there and shine!

Index

www.ingramcontent.com/pod-product-compliance
Lightning Source LLC
Chambersburg PA
CBHW031412150726
47989CB00002B/627